DANCING THE *Spirituals*
...AN AMAZING GRACE

AN INSTRUCTIONAL GUIDE TO INTRODUCING AFRICAN AMERICAN SPIRITUALS TO YOUR CONGREGATION THROUGH DANCE

BY SYLVIA BUCK BRYANT

Dancing the Spirituals...An Amazing Grace
Published 2016.

Cover Photo: Singing Windows stained glass, designed by JR Lamb, located in the University chapel at Tuskegee University, Tuskegee, Alabama The George F. Landegger Collection of Alabama Photographs in Carol M. Highsmith's America, Library of Congress, Prints and Photographs Division.

The lyrics of the spirituals in this book were taken from: *Songs of Zion*. Nashville, TN: Abingdon, 1981. Print.

Photography by Susie Adamson, Julian Espinal and Diana Sherblom

ISBN: 978-0-692-67677-6

ADVANCE PRAISE

FOR *DANCING THE SPIRITUALS... AN AMAZING GRACE*

Dancing the Spirituals incorporates two essential elements in the history of worship that are often neglected and even condemned for their potential as praise — dance and spiritual song. Sylvia Bryant not only gives African-American spirituals a new hearing, she ensures that they will be *seen* and *felt* in a new way. This book will help ministers and lay people alike bring the spirituals to life in their own congregations.
—William B McClain, *Professor of Preaching and Worship, Wesley Theological Seminary*

"In the world of dance as a sacred art, Sylvia Bryant is a giant! She brings a clear and focused energy that inspires and humbles those who move with her and audiences alike. Her presence is at once huge and insistent while also leaving one contemplative and reflective. Her gifts are many; we are so fortunate to have her in our community."
—Wendy Morrell, *President, Sacred Dance Guild*

"Sylvia's passionate performance at Paa Ya Paa Arts Centre in 2014 revealed her great talent as a cultural ambassador for the renowned African American Spirituals on an international stage. I am thrilled to know these compositions will continue to help the human spirit soar.
—Elimo Njau, *Artist, Founder & Director, Paa Ya Paa Arts Centre, Nairobi, Kenya*

"*Dancing the Spirituals* incorporates poetry, music, dance and drama with simple, illustrated movements to express the depth of the African American Spirituals and tap their power to nourish the human soul. This book will be very useful to all age groups looking for fresh ways keep the Spirituals relevant in today's world!"
—Phillda Ragland Njau, *International Arts Program Coordinator, Paa Ya Paa Arts Centre, Nairobi, Kenya*

"When I dance, it comes from the deepest part of my soul, where my heart is open and my spirit is free. When I jump, I am reaching for my ancestors in heaven. Dance connects us to our history, our legacy, our inner spirit, and to God. To harness your troubles and let your soul physically move you is dance's great gift."
—Arcell Cabuag, *Associate Artistic Director & Dancer,*
RONALD K. BROWN/ EVIDENCE, A DANCE COMPANY, *Brooklyn, NY*

"Sylvia Bryant's liturgical dance is a conduit for grace to flow throughout our church's worship services; it inspires our bodies to not only sit and stand, but joyfully dance and jump in the Spirit of the Lord."
—Reverend Earl Kim, *First United Methodist Church of Montclair, New Jersey*

"This song, dance, moan, groan and shout is our heritage passed down so that future generations will not only create spirituals, but continue to be proud of them. *Amazing Grace* is the voice of our very soul. I challenge you, "nothing but an echo of the past, yet I am the ethical of the future. How will I ever know where to go, if I don't know where I've been?""
—Reverend Dr. Verolga Nix , *Historian/Musician of African American Music*

"Liturgical dance is an intimate conversation with God. When the music ends, I am changed—whatever burdens I was carrying have been lifted."
—Rochelle Wilson, *"The Call to Worship Ensemble"*

FOR WILLIAM "SONNY" MATTHEW PALMER BUCK JR.— my big brother, and my spiritual rock. Sonny was an outstanding professional jazz musician, strong in faith, and a pillar of his Catholic community. He generously shared his gift of music with everyone who knew him. He often encouraged me to share my gift of dance with a larger audience by writing a historic book such as this. This book is for you, Sonny. Your beautiful legacy will never be forgotten.

TABLE OF CONTENTS

AFRICAN AMERICAN SPIRITUALS, LITURGICAL DANCE AND THE RELIGIOUS EXPERIENCE; MAKING CONNECTIONS IN TODAY'S WORLD

Foreward	ix
Introduction	xi
Best Practices	xiii
Ev'ry Time I Feel the Spirit	1
My Lord! What a Mourning	7
I Want to be Ready	15
Let Us Break Bread Together	21
Kum Ba Yah, My Lord	27
Wade in the Water	33
Go Tell It on the Mountain	39
Oh, Freedom	47
He's Got the Whole World in His Hands	55
Go Down Moses	61
Acknowledgements	71
About the Author	73
About the Illustrator	75

FOREWORD

AFRICAN AMERICAN SPIRITUALS, LITURGICAL DANCE AND THE RELIGIOUS EXPERIENCE; MAKING CONNECTIONS IN TODAY'S WORLD

THE SOUL-STIRRING HARMONIES OF THE AFRICAN AMERICAN SPIRITUALS ARE A TESTAMENT TO THE INDOMITABLE HUMAN SPIRIT OF THE ENSLAVED AFRICANS IN THE U.S. Rooted in biblical passages and liberation theology, they have transcended their humble origins to become the sacred songs that comfort and inspire oppressed people in their struggles all over the world. They have particular relevance today, as discrimination, police brutality and injustice continue to plague our own society.

As liturgical dancers and praise dance groups, how can we help the spirituals resonate in contemporary worship services? *Dancing the Spirituals; an Amazing Grace* is a comprehensive guide to bringing the spirituals songs to life through creative movement and dance for all generations and denominations.

My deep love of the African American spirituals came from my mother, Laura Buck McCray. The Assistant Dean of Students at Tuskegee University in Tuskegee, Alabama, my mother used to take my brothers and me to the University's chapel to see the Singing Windows — eleven stained glass windows, each portraying the story of a spiritual. My mother was a tremendous storyteller; she used to sit us down below the windows to tell us their stories. Some of her favorites were "Go Down Moses," "Swing Low, Sweet Chariot" and "Rise Up Shepherds." I learned the history of slavery through those windows, and they left an indelible mark on my life.

At 18 years old, I was a passionate dancer trained in ballet, modern, jazz and African dance, when my mother asked me to choreograph and perform at a graduation ceremony for the Buck-McCray School of Business (which she founded and directed). The ceremony was to be held in the sanctuary of our church (the Greenwood Missionary Baptist Church). At the time, nobody danced in church—and certainly not to secular music. I was at a loss for what to do when my mother suggested that I choreograph one of her favorite spirituals, "My Lord, What a Mourning." Interpreting that song—which illustrates a dark chapter of African American history—sparked my interest in exploring the creative potential of liturgical choreography.

My passion didn't take flight, however, until I married my husband, the late Rev. Fletcher J. Bryant. An outstanding United Methodist minister, Fletcher supported my interest in bringing sacred dance to our church community. The community embraced it as well, which led to a career of choreographing, teaching and performing liturgical dance in parishes, festivals and schools all over the world.

Compiling *Dancing the Spirituals* has been a decades long passion, and a gift from God. I hope that these compositions will continue to inspire and move other congregations for years to come. Dancers of all abilities can access the straightforward choreography, illustrations and video demonstrations—enthusiasm can be a great substitute for training. I encourage you to bring the spirituals to life in your house of worship, and to dance with amazing grace!

INTRODUCTION

AFRICAN AMERICAN SPIRITUALS, LITURGICAL DANCE AND THE RELIGIOUS EXPERIENCE; MAKING THE CONNECTION TODAY

THE SPIRITUALS ARE A RICH, ESSENTIAL PART OF AFRICAN AMERICAN HISTORY, YET THEY STRUGGLE TO BE RELEVANT TO YOUNGER EARS. Creative expression - dance, art, music, and spoken word – has always engaged new audiences by allowing room for reinterpretation and participation. Time and time again, I have witnessed the power of dance to awaken ancient texts and reach multigenerational audiences, in worship services and secular performances alike. This book contains practical steps and accessible choreography to help contemporary dancers bring ten historic spirituals to life today, and for future generations. Don't let the inspiration and power of these sacred songs be lost. I encourage you to incorporate these spirituals into your worship service during black history and women's history month, and at other times throughout the year.

Who should read this book?
This manual is designed for liturgical and praise dance groups of all ages, faiths, and ethnicities. Whether you are a dancer or simply an interested party, you will find the choreography accessible and highly expressive — evocative of the history and experience of early African-Americans.

BRINGING DANCE TO YOUR WORSHIP COMMUNITY

AS THE COORDINATOR RESPONSIBLE FOR BRINGING THESE COMPOSITIONS TO YOUR CONGREGATION, TREAT THE PROCESS AS YOU WOULD A PROFESSIONAL ASSIGNMENT. Bring your best work to the process, from the planning and coordination to the execution of the dance. Consult these suggestions to plan and execute a successful worship experience.

1) Get leadership buy-in
Before embarking on a project of this magnitude, approach your congregation's minister (or leader) and the music director with your proposal. Begin by explaining why incorporating the danced African American spirituals into your worship services is particularly meaningful (see the introduction for more on that). Once the idea is approved, consult the church's calendar to determine appropriate spirituals for specific services and events throughout the year.

2) Bring in dancers.
As the choreography interpreter and teacher, the dance director should have a thorough understanding of dance technique. Invite interested participants, and consider including all ages and genders so that the dance can truly reflect the diversity of your congregation. Hold a master class to teach participants the principals of sacred and liturgical dance before tackling the choreography. Most of the dances are appropriate for anywhere from one to 12 dancers.

3) Partner with the musical director.
These compositions can work with a range of accompaniments, from a soloist to a choir, spoken word, drums, and/or a variety of instruments. Ask the director of music ministry for her expertise in musical selection, and to coordinate the music rehearsals. Because the dancers will need to rehearse more, request a recording of the music to economize the musicians' rehearsal time.

4) Practice, and invite critiques.
Coordinate rehearsal time with leadership, ideally in the area where the dance will be performed (the chancel, normally). Midway through rehearsals, invite the minister and technical director to sit in for a critique. You may want to videotape the session to help articulate any suggested changes.

5) Plan for participation.
On occasion, parishioners are moved to share in the dance, and it can be a spiritual, uplifting experience. If you want to encourage audience participation, specify it in advance. Ask for the service bulletin to include a note inviting congregants to participate as a form of worship, rather than viewing it as a performance.

6) Connect with resources.
You aren't alone in your appreciation of and desire to promote worship through dance. For support, information, fellowship and advocacy of sacred and liturgical dance, contact The Fellowship of United Methodists in Music and Worship Arts (*www.umfellowship.org*) and The Sacred Dance Guild (*sacreddanceguild.org*).

EV'RY TIME I FEEL THE SPIRIT

Feel the spirit, fire and smoke, body chills not the soul, every time in the heart…pray.

EV'RY TIME I FEEL THE SPIRIT

Refrain:

Ev'ry time I feel the spirit moving in my heart
I will pray.

Verse 1:

Upon the mountain when my Lord spoke,
Out his mouth came fire and smoke.
All around me look so shine,
Ask my Lord if all was mine.

Refrain:

Verse 2:

Jordan River is chilly and cold,
Chills the body but not the soul.
Ain't but one train on dis' track,
runs to heaven and right back.

Refrain:

Recommendations:
One to ten dancers, accompanied by ensemble, piano, organ or drums. Tempo is fast and rhythmic, mood upbeat and spirited. Dancers may also hold a drum or tambourine.

Refrain:

Ev'ry Time I Feel the Spirit Moving in My Heart, I will pray. (2 times)

Dancers walk forward with a step/tap (step on one foot, tap the other near it) while swaying side to side and clapping hands vigorously in front of face (or playing an instrument). **(fig. 1)** On "pray," bring hands to prayer position, lean back and face up.

**Figure 1
Dancers with instruments**

Figure 2
Hands in calling position

Figure 4
Floating hands

Verse 1:

Upon the mountain when my Lord spoke

Dancers run from sides to face a partner in the center. Touch hands overhead, then turn back-to-back, placing hands in a calling position above the mouth, then extending them up. **(fig. 2)**

Figure 3
Pulsing hands

out his mouth came fire and smoke.

Dancers turn in individual circles, patting down and pulsing hands to represent fire and smoke. **(fig. 3)**

All around me look so shine, ask my Lord…

Dancers move around chancel in a triplet walk, alternating between a crouch, medium and high, while hands float in space. **(fig. 4)** On "ask my Lord," dancers fall softly to floor, then rise.

… if all was mine.

Dancers rise while lifting arms forward, then up to ceiling. Then slowly contract; head down, knees bent, arms wrapped around themselves. (**fig. 5**)

Refrain:

Repeat refrain choreography.

Verse 2:

Jordan River is chilly and cold,

Dancers walk in a small circle, swinging arms in a wave-like movement. (**fig. 6**)

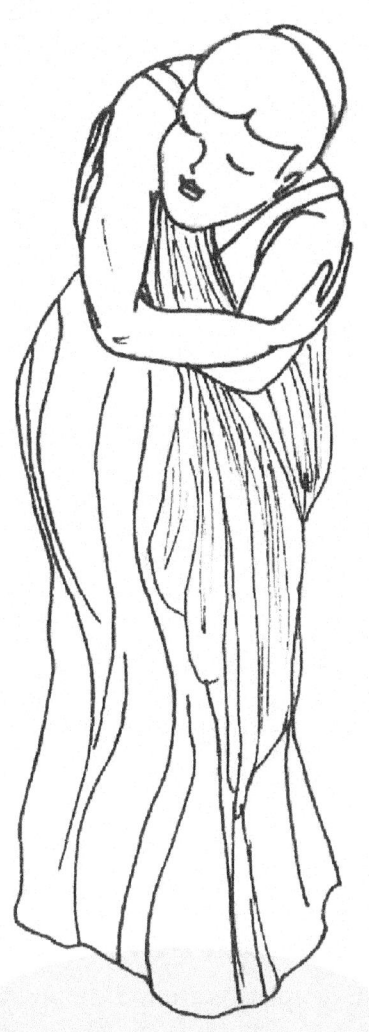

**Figure 5
Self-embrace**

**Figure 6
Swinging arms**

Figure 7
Warm the body

Figure 8
Kneeling in prayer

chills the body but not the soul.

With head down, wrap arms around shoulders (**fig. 7**) as though warming the body. On "not the soul", drop to the left knee, (**fig. 8**) swing arms back and around to prayer position, and look up.

Ain't but one train on dis track, runs to heaven and right back.

Moving arms and legs in a locomotive motion (while lowering and raising body), circle to the right. On "runs to heaven," dancers lift left arm straight above head, palm facing forward. Lower it until palm is next to face. On "right back," flex left hand and push forward. (**fig. 9**)

Figure 9
Arm extended

MY LORD! WHAT A MOURNING

That day when finally the Lord comes with deliverance— from torment to triumph. What a morning!

MY LORD! WHAT A MOURNING

My Lord! What a mourning.
My Lord! What a mourning.
Yes, my Lord what a mourning,
when the stars begin to fall.

Verse 1:

You'll hear the trumpet sound
to wake the nations underground.
Looking to my God's right-hand
when the stars begin to fall.

Verse 2:

You'll hear the sinner cry
to wake the nations underground.
Looking to my God's right hand
when the stars begin to fall.

Verse 3:

You'll hear the Christian shout
to wake the nations underground.
Looking to my God's right hand
when the stars begin to fall.

Recommendations:
One to 10 dancers accompanied by a choir, soloist or ensemble. Tempo is slow, movements lyrical.
Note: *Refrain choreography is numbered, and repeated in some verses.*

Starting position:
Facing the congregation, arms rounded in front of contracted body, head focuses on hands. **(fig. 1)**

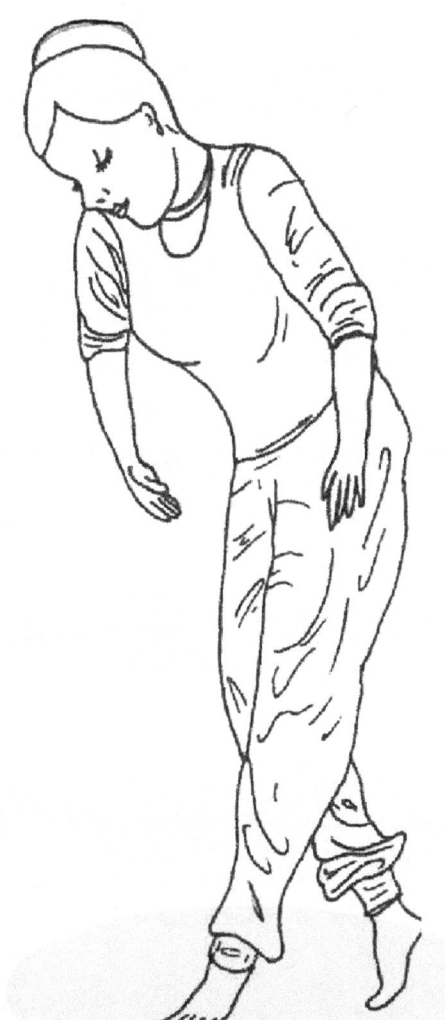

Figure 1
Arms round in front of body

Refrain:

* *Refrain step 1:*

My Lord! What a mourning (2x)
(first right, then left side)

Sweep right foot out to the side, ending in a deep lunge (right knee bent), while also swinging arms and head up to the same side. **(fig. 2)** On "morning," lower arms in four pulsating movements, ending with arms open wide near hips, palms and head facing up. **(fig. 3)**

* *Refrain step 2:*

Figure 2
Side lunge, raised arms and head

Figure 3
Head focuses up

Yes, my Lord what a mourning

Step forward with the right foot and swing arms up (head follows arm movements) while sweeping left leg forward into a turned out position. In the same movement, take a small jump on the left foot. **(fig. 4)**

* Refrain step 3:

When the stars begin to fall

Lower straight arms to floor while fluttering fingers to indicate falling stars, then lay down on right side, with fingers and toes pointed, so the body forms a straight line. **(fig. 5)**

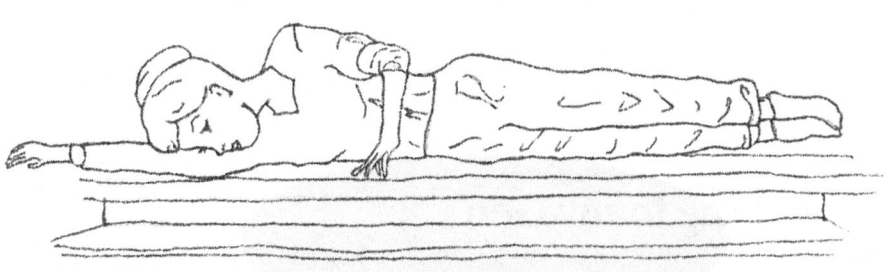

Figure 5
Body forms a line

Figure 4
Turned out leap

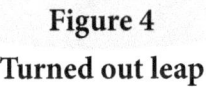

You'll hear the trumpet sound

Dancers rise to knees, step right foot forward and turn slightly right while framing ears with extended hands and arms that push out. **(fig. 6)**. On "sound," clap hands overhead and look up.

Figure 6
Kneeling, arms extended

to wake the nation's underground.
Keeping arms close to torso, lift them above shoulders and round into a forward contraction, arms dangling over bent knees. **(figs. 7a, 7b)**

Looking to my God's

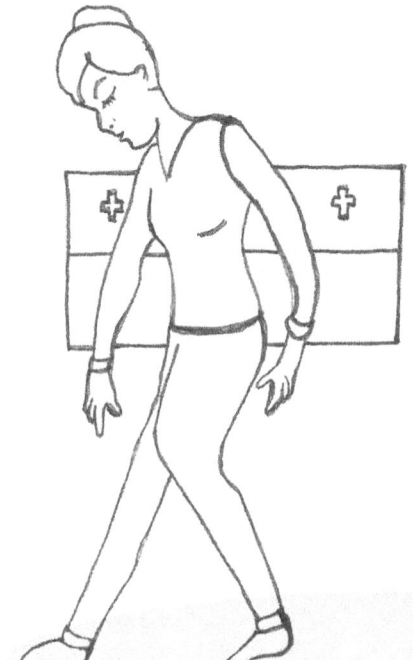

Figure 7a
Rounding shoulders

Figure 7b
Forward bent torso

right hand
Repeat refrain step 2 choreography.

when the stars begin to fall.
Repeat refrain step 3 choreography.

Figure 8
Hands frame face

Verse 2:

You'll hear the sinner cry
Step forward on the left, then right foot to bring feet together. Torso is bent slightly forward, and hands create a frame in front of the face with palms facing out and fingers extended. Round and lower the torso further in four quick, short pulsating movements. **(fig. 8)**

to wake the nation's underground.
Keeping arms close to torso, lift them above shoulders and round into a forward contraction, with arms dangling over bent knees. **(fig. 7b)**

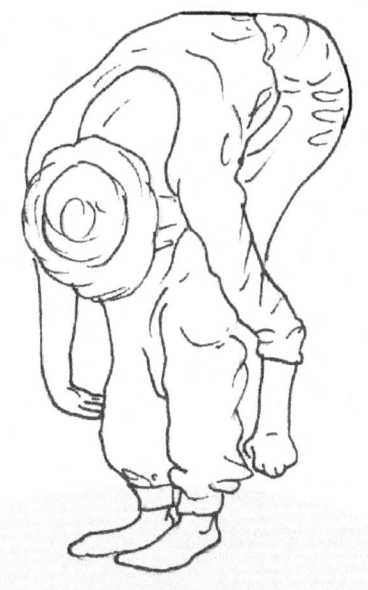

Figure 7b
Forward bent torso

Looking to my God's right hand
Repeat refrain step 2 choreography.

when the stars begin to fall.
Repeat refrain step 3 choreography.

Verse 3:

You'll hear the Christians shout to wake the nation's underground.
Dancers clap and step rhythmically and joyfully around the chancel, incorporating improvisational movements. **(fig. 9)**

Figures 9a, 9b
Dancers clap and move around chancel

Look into my God's right hand

Cross the right foot over left to make a complete left turn, then jump on right foot, swing right arm up, and swing left bent leg forward and left arm to the side. (**fig. 10**)

when the stars begin to fall.

Facing right and leading with rounded arms, dancers take a full low right turn before leaping onto right leg. On landing, dancers take positions for the closing pose, which can be adapted according to the number of dancers (several groups, for example). (**fig. 11**)

Figure 10
Swing right arm up, left leg out

Back Dancer: Positioned behind middle dancer, torso leaning back slightly, right leg straight, left leg fully extended off the ground above the middle dancer's left foot. Both arms are fully extended, with left hand in front of forehead and the right hand touching (from above) the other dancer's arms.

Middle Dancer: Left foot is forward, right leg in a slight plié, both heels slightly off the floor. Back is straight with right arm wrapped around the front dancer's right arm, and left hand outstretched above the front dancer's.

Figure 11
Dancers in final pose

Front Dancer: stands on toes in a deep lunge with pelvis forward, torso back, and right arm wrapped around middle dancer's elbow. Left hand reaches up and forward.

✸ I WANT TO BE READY ✸

*From despair to joy, to walking in
Jersualem with Jesus, just like John. Joy!*

I WANT TO BE READY

Refrain:

I want to be ready,
I want to be ready
I want to be ready
to walk in Jerusalem just like John

Verse 1:

O John, O John, what do you say?
Walk in Jerusalem just like John
That I'll be there at the coming day
Walk in Jerusalem just like John

Refrain:

Verse 2:

John said the city was just four-square
Walk in Jerusalem just like John
And he declared he'd meet me there
Walk in Jerusalem just like John

Refrain:

Recommendations: Tempo is fast and upbeat, mood spirited. Up to 12 dancers enter from the sides, moving in different directions around the chancel during the refrain.

Refrain:

I want to be ready (2x)
Take a small leap on the left foot while raising the opposite hand and tapping the right foot near the left. **(fig. 1)**
Repeat on the other side.

Figure 1
Step and raise opposite hand

Figure 2
Arm leads a walking circle

I want to be ready

Step with the left foot, then walk in a circle to the right, leading with right arm. Left arm is in a half circle down the side, not touching the body. **(fig. 2)**

to walk in Jerusalem just like John.*

*repeat this choreography every verse

Step with the right foot, then leading with left arm, walk in a circle to the left. Right arm is in a semi circle down the side, not touching body. **(fig. 2)**

Verse 1:

O John, O John, What Do You Say?

With hands on hips, bend right, then left on each "John", head down (as if talking to someone). **(fig. 3a)** On "what do you say," step forward in a right lunge and point up. **(fig. 3b)**

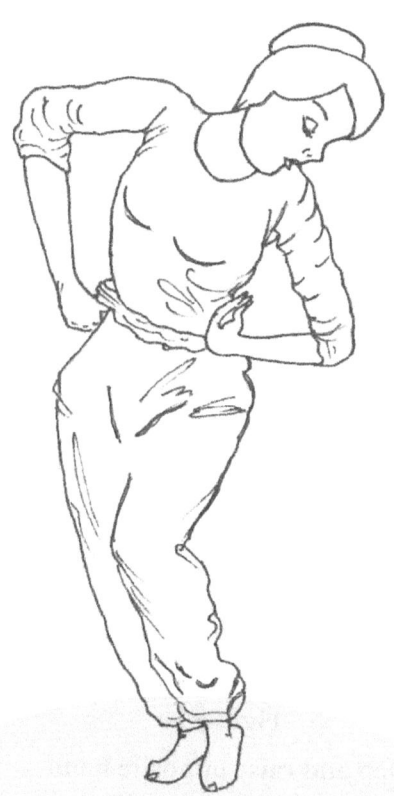

Figure 3a
Bend side to side

Figure 3b
Right lunge, pointing up

Walk in Jerusalem just like John
Repeat refrain choreography (fig. 2).

That'll be there ...
Step forward with the right foot, bringing the left foot behind it while rocking forward with rounded torso, and swinging arms and head forward so they hang down over knees. (**fig. 5**)

Figure 5
Head hanging to knees

... at the coming Day
In a quick forceful movement, open arms wide to shoulder level, straighten back, and focus head up. (**fig. 6**)

Figure 6
Arms wide, facing up

Figure 7
Leap right, then left

Figure 8
Dancers greet and shake hands

Walk in Jerusalem, just like John.
Repeat last line of refrain choreography (**fig. 2**).

Refrain:
Repeat entire refrain choreography

Verse 2:

John said the city was just four square
Leading with right foot, take two big leaps to the right, then two to the left. (**fig. 7**)

Walk in Jerusalem, just like John.
Repeat last line of refrain choreography (**fig. 2**)

and He declared He'd meet me there.
Dancers move quickly in different directions all over the chancel, shaking hands and greeting one another. (**fig. 8**)

To walk in Jerusalem just like John
Repeat last line of refrain choreography (**fig. 2**).

Refrain:
- *End the last line a joyous leap.*

LET US BREAK BREAD TOGETHER

Verse 1:

Let us break bread together on our knees.
Let us break bread together on our knees.

Refrain:

When I fall on my knees
With my face to the rising sun
Oh, Lord, have mercy on me.

Verse 2:

Let us drink wine together on our knees.
Let us drink wine together on our knees.

Refrain:

Verse 3:

Let us praise God together on our knees.
Let us praise god together on our knees.

Refrain:

Recommendations:
Up to 12 dancers, slow tempo, lyrical movements.

Verse 1:

Let us break bread together on our knees (2x)

Holding hands in front of chest, walk towards the congregation. Make a sharp breaking motion on "break," then extend arms in a large outward circle, as though making an offering. On "knees," round shoulders and arms forward as if diving, placing hands on the knees. *(figs. 1 and 2)*

Figure 1
Separate hands on "break bread"

Figure 2
Rounding over the knees

Figure 4
Bent towards floor

When I fall on my knees

Focusing on floor, dancers round forward into a demi-plié and tap knees quickly with hands. **(fig. 4)**

Figure 5
Head focused on ceiling

with my face to the rising sun

Facing up with arms softly at sides **(fig.5)**, dancers stand on toes and cross left foot over right to spin to the right. Then fall on the floor to the right, extending hands overhead **(fig. 6)**. Rise quickly to stand again with feet apart, hands clasped above chest, torso and shoulders leaning back slightly, facing up. **(fig. 7)**

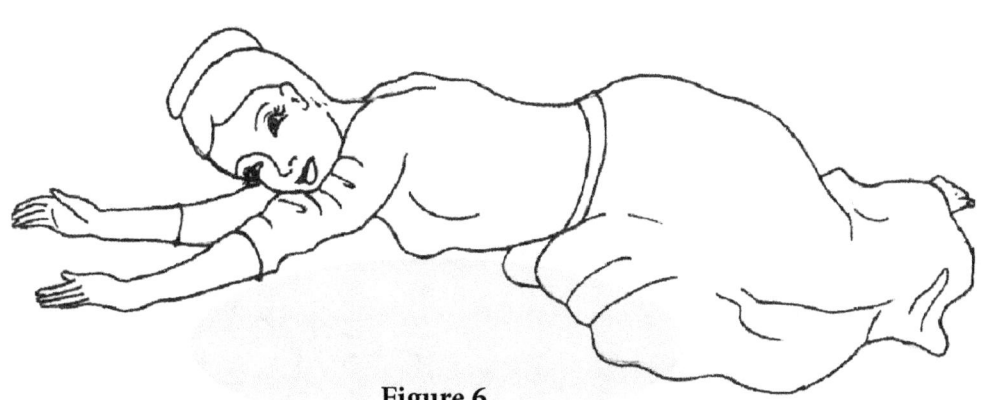

Figure 6
Lying down, hands extended

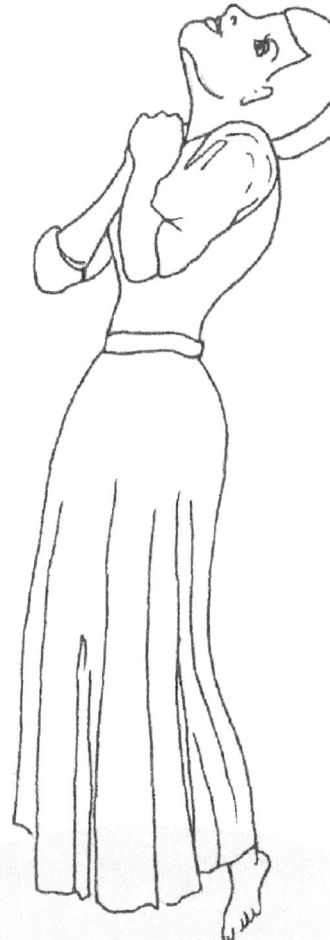

Figure 7
Facing the rising sun

Figure 8
Circle the arms

Oh Lord, have mercy on me

Dancers walk in a circle to the right, forcefully swinging arms (also in a right turning circle) then lunge right, torso leaning back, hands together in front of chest, facing up. **(figs. 8, 9)**

Figure 9
Cross arms in front of chest

Figure 10
Scooping a cup

Verse 2:
Let us drink wine together (2x)

Dancers reach down as though scooping a cup, **(fig. 10)** then stand to bring it to their mouth. **(fig. 11)**

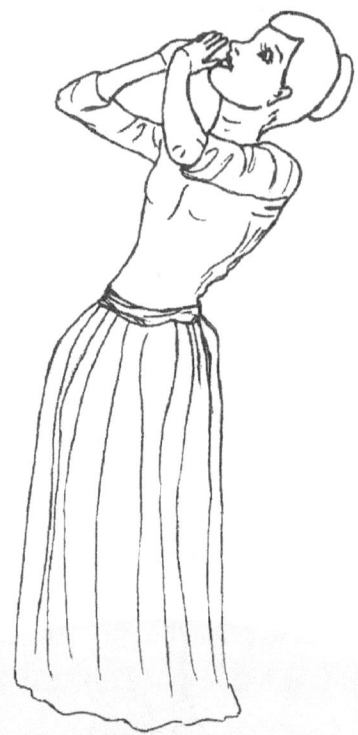

Figure 11
Drinking from the cup

Refrain:

Verse 3:
Let us praise God together on our knees (2x)

Dancers take long, deep lunges forward, twisting the torso, head, and lifting the opposite arms as the front leg leading each stride. **(fig. 12)**

Refrain:

Figure 12
Arms overhead

⚜ KUM BA YAH, MY LORD ⚜

Feel the heart of slaves gathered. Come by here Lord, deliver... we pray, we cry, we sing, we praise!

KUM BA YAH

Verse 1:

Kum ba yah, my Lord, kum ba yah
Kum ba yah, my Lord, kum ba yah
Kum ba yah, my Lord, kum ba yah
Oh Lord, kum ba yah

Verse 2:

Someone's crying, Lord….. kum ba yah (3x)
Oh Lord, kum ba yah

Verse 3:

Someone's singing, Lord…. kum ba yah (3x)
Oh Lord, kum ba yah

Verse 4:

Someone's praying, Lord…. kum ba yah. (3x)
Oh Lord, kum ba yah

Recommendations:
*Up to 12 dancers, upbeat tempo, rhythm is an African-inspired syncopated triplet. Percussive instruments accompany. Dancers enter chancel through center and side aisles with a quick shuffle step. Singing begins when dancers are in **starting position:** Torsos rounded, knees bent, head and fingers hanging to floor.*

Verse 1:

Kum ba yah, my Lord, kum ba yah (3x)

With bent knees and rounded torso, dancers move in small rocking shuffle steps (1-2-3 to the right, 1-2-3- to the left). Both hands reach down as if scooping from the floor on alternating sides. **(fig. 1)**

**Figure 1
Scooping from one side**

Figure 2
In releve, push hands up

Oh, Lord, kum ba yah
(*repeat this choreography for every verse)
Lunge forward, slowly bringing arms overhead. Then rise onto toes (in relevé), flex and push hands up in one sustained movement. **(fig. 2)**

Verse 2:

Someone's crying Lord, kum ba yah (3x)
Starting over the face, lower the right hand with wiggling fingers down the torso. **(fig. 3)** Continue downward movement, bending forward until head almost touches slightly bent knees and both hands are next to the knees, facing up, cupped, on "kum ba yah."

Oh, Lord, kum ba yah
Repeat choreography (fig 2).

Figure 3
Lowering right hand

Verse 3:
Someone's singing Lord, kum ba yah (3x)

Moving backwards into a cluster, dancers cup hands in a calling position, then extend the arms outward (on each repetition, alternate direction of arms: to the left, right, then straight) **(figs. 4, 5)**

Figure 4
Cupping hands

Figure 5
Extending arms to one side

Oh, Lord, kum ba yah
Repeat choreography. (fig. 2)

Figure 2
In releve, push hands up

Verse 4:

Someone's praying lord, kum ba yah (3x)

With wide arms and feet, dancers turn right to face away from the congregation. On "kum ba yah," clap hands and raise them above head. Dancers face congregation for the second line, and turn away again for the last.

(figs. 6, 7)

Figure 6
Turning with wide arms and feet

Figure 7
Hands in prayer above head

Oh, Lord, Kum Ba Yah
Repeat choreography. (fig. 2)

Figure 2
In releve, push hands up

❋ WADE IN THE WATER ❋

Wade in the water with the Underground Railroad. Deliverance belongs to God's children; God's gonna trouble the water.

WADE IN THE WATER

Refrain:

Wade in the water
Wade in the water children
Wade in the water
God's agonna trouble the water

Verse 1:

See that band all dressed in white?
God's agonna trouble the water
The leader looks like an Israelite.
God's agonna trouble the water

Verse 2:

See the band all dressed in red
God's agonna trouble the water
It looks like the band that Moses led.
God's agonna trouble the water

Refrain:

Recommendations:
Up to 12 dancers, upbeat tempo with soulful, lyrical movements. Props: pitcher, large water bowl, fabrics (15 to 20 foot-long swaths of cloth) in blue, white and red.

Starting Position:
One dancer enters through the center aisle with a pitcher of water. **(fig. 1)** After pouring it into a bowl on the chancel, she walks to the side. **(fig 2)**

Figure 1
Carrying a vessel

One or two dancers run down the aisle moving a long blue cloth up and down overhead so it ripples and flows. Others dance alongside, making wave-like movements with arms and body. At the center of the chancel, the leader wraps the cloth and puts it to one side. **(fig. 3)**

Figure 2
Pouring water into the bowl

Figure 3
Moving the cloth up and down

Refrain:

this refrain choreography repeats throughout the song.

Wade in the water
Wade in the water children.
Wade in the water

Dancers move toward one another in deep pliés, dropping their torsos as they lunge right and left until they join hands in a line. **(fig. 4)**

Figure 4
Linking Hands

God's agonna trouble the water.

Dancers move in a (1-2-3) shuffle with deeply bent knees, rounded shoulders, and arms making wave-like movements – alternating left and right sides as they move towards one another in a large circle. **(fig. 5)**

Figure 5
Troubling the water

Verse 1:

See that band all dressed in white

Dancers lunge right with hands covering face, palms out. They pull hands apart to reveal face as a new dancer(s) runs down the aisle holding a white cloth overhead. **(figs. 6a, 6b)**

God's agonna trouble the water.

Repeat refrain choreography **(fig. 5)** while leader folds the white cloth and puts it to the side.

Figures 6a, 6b
Troubling the water

Figure 7
Dancer leads the others

Figure 5
Troubling the water

The leader looks like an Israelite.
Repeat refrain choreography (fig.5) while the leader stands up tall in the middle of the group, extends the right arm up and takes four steps backward (leading with the right leg) while focusing up past the arm. (**fig. 7**)

God's agonna trouble the water
Repeat refrain choreography (fig.5), while the leader returns to the group.

Verse 2:

See the band all dressed in red
A new dancer runs down the center aisle with a red cloth (**fig. 3**) while chancel dancers lunge right, pulling their hands away from their face (palms out). (**figs. 6a, 6b**) When the leader arrives on the chancel, dancers start to cluster around her.

Gods agonna trouble the water
Repeat refrain choreography (**fig. 5**) while contracting and bending knees towards the center leader, with arms overhead.

It looks like the band that Moses led.
Leader stands up in the center of the cluster, holding the red cloth high in her right hand. (**fig.7**) She walks with hip-led rhythmic movement in a large circle to the left, leading dancers, who unfurl from the cluster one by one as they follow.

God's agonna trouble the water
Dancers repeat refrain choreography as they exit.(fig. 5)

Refrain:
Dancers move in a fluid cluster, dancing down center and side aisles, making wave-like movements as they exit.

GO TELL IT ON THE MOUNTAIN

Refrain:

Go, tell it on the mountain
over the hills and everywhere.
Go, tell it on the mountain
that Jesus Christ is born.

Verse 1:

While shepherds kept their watching
o'er Silent flocks by night.
Behold throughout the heavens
there shone a holy light.

Refrain:

Verse 2:

The shepherds feared and trembled when lo' above the earth
rang out the Angel chorus that hailed our Savior's birth.

Refrain:

Verse 3:

Down in lowly manger the humble Christ was born
and God sent us salvation that blessed Christmas morn.

Recommendations:
Up to 12 dancers. Highly spirited, upbeat, and soulful. Vary accompaniments with African drums or other percussive instruments.

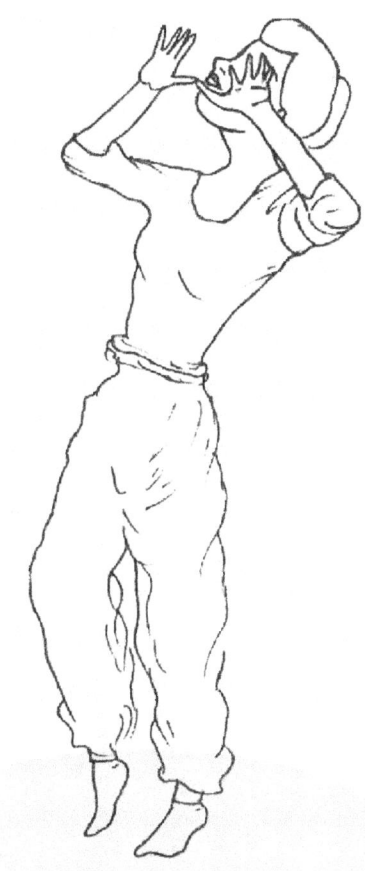

Figure 1
Cup hands to call

Refrain:
*To be repeated

Go, tell it on the mountain

Alternate right and left leaps (4 times).
With each leap, cup hands then
extend arms up. **(fig.1)**

over the hills and everywhere.

Lift arms to shoulders and contract forward, folding over bent knees. (**fig. 2**) On "everywhere," swing out arms forcefully, alternating left and ride side, high and low, using all available space. (**fig. 3**)

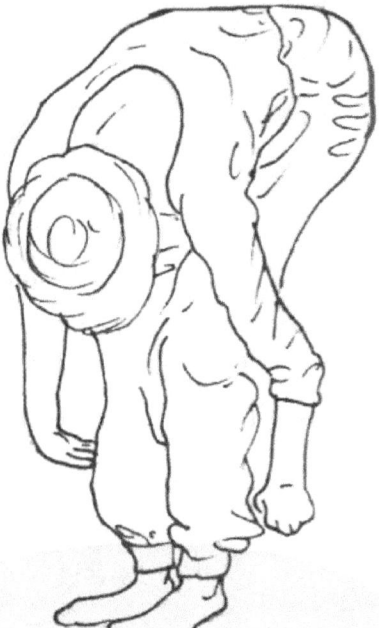

Figure 2
Bent torso

Figure 3
Swing arms wide

Go, tell it on the mountain

Alternate right and left leaps (4x). With each leap, cup hands in front mouth, then extend arms up. (**fig. 1**)

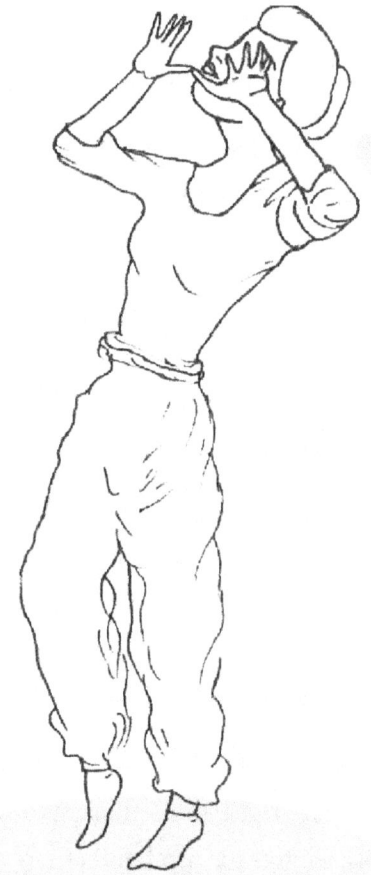

Figure 9.4
Push arms up to the right

that Jesus Christ

Beginning with bent knees, leap and sweep arms up to the right as if pushing the air. **(fig. 4)**

is born.

With feet together and bent knees, cradle arms on the left side, and circle torso, head and arms counterclockwise. **(fig. 5)**

While shepherds kept their watching

Take two long strides—leading with the right foot, twisting right and turning head down as arms swing out to the right at shoulder height. On "kept their watching," the left foot is forward, and arms, head and torso swing up to the left. **(figs. 6 and 7)**

Figures 4 and 5
Sweep arms up, cradle

Figure 6
Twisting right stride

Figure 7
Twisting left stride

Figure 8
Sweeping circle with extended arms

o'er silent flock by night

Dancers sweep outstretched arms in a semicircle from left to right while completing a circle to the right. **(fig. 8)** On "night," leap right and bend in a deep contraction (facing side, not front).

behold throughout the heavens, there shone a holy light.

From the contraction, sweep left leg up and to the left, turning to face front, landing in second position, arms away from the body. Lift arms overhead and lower them to hips in small, quick, pulsating movements. **(fig. 9)**

Figure 9
Lower arms with pulsating movements

Refrain:
Repeat refrain choreography

Verse 2:

The shepherds feared and trembled
With legs wide, extend trembling arms and hands overhead then stand in relevé. **(fig. 10)**

when lo' above the earth
Slowly lower arms, rounding body until fully contracted with bent knees, head down and hands touching the floor. **(fig. 11)**

Figure 10
Lift trembling arms

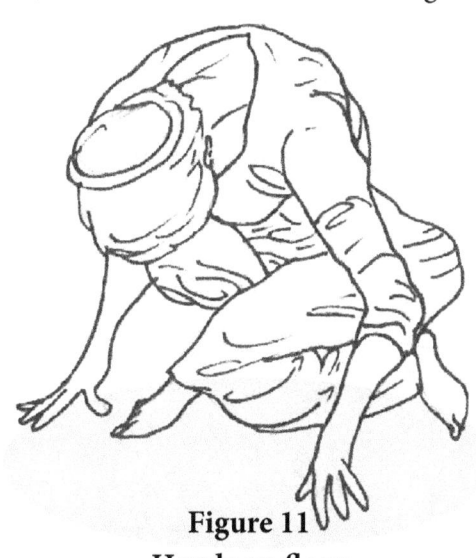

Figure 11
Hands on floor

rang out the angel chorus
Stand up to swing entire body left to right, leading with arms and bending knees deeply between swings. **(figs. 12, 13)**

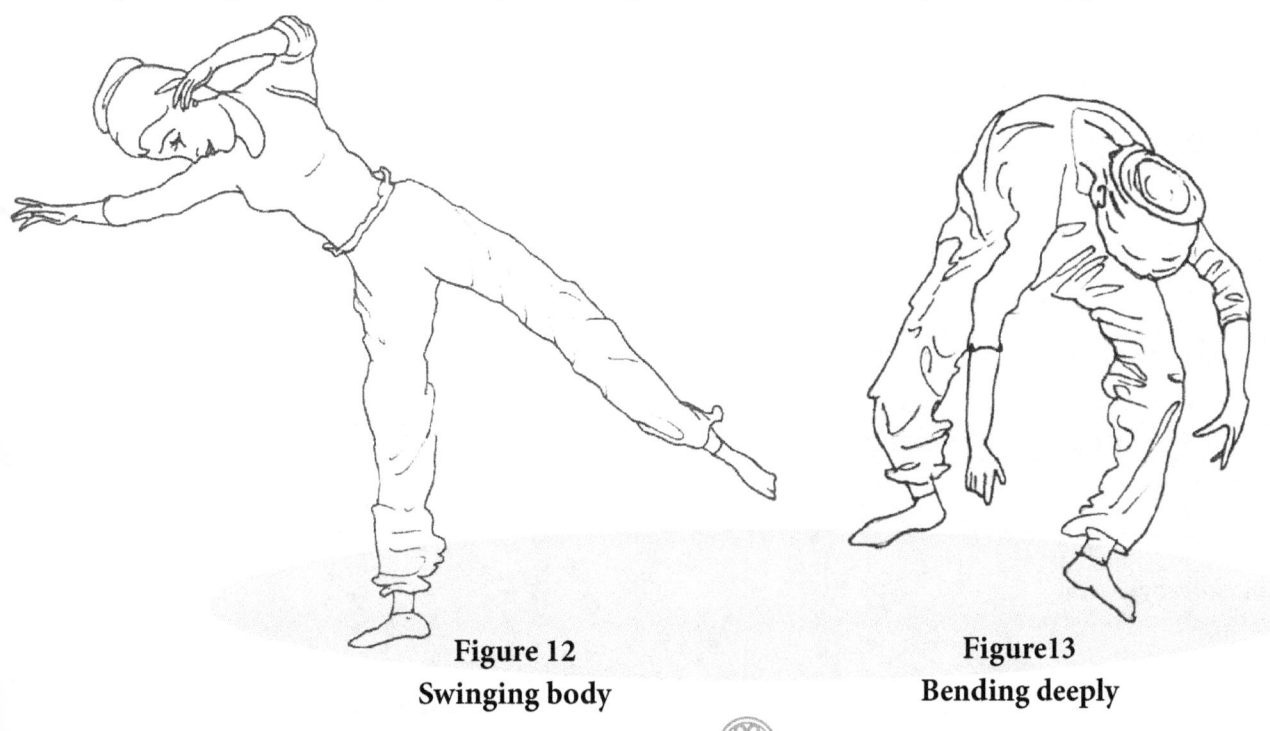

Figure 12
Swinging body

Figure 13
Bending deeply

that hailed our Savior's birth.

Gently lower both knees to floor, extend arms out at chest height with cupped hands, then slowly lift them until hands are overhead. (**fig. 14**)

Refrain:

***Repeat refrain choreography**

**Figure 14
Outstretched hands**

Verse 3:

Down in a lowly manger

Dancers walk to the chancel's edge, face the congregation and fall softly to their knees as they lean on their inside hand and stretch the opposite arm overhead towards the center. (**fig. 15**)

the humble Christ was born

Dancers kneel and place hands in lap. (**fig. 16**)

and God sent us salvation

Dancers rise and walk in their own small circle to the right.

that blessed Christmas morn.

Dancers run to the center of the chancel, interlock arms to form a large circle, and take small steps to the right, looking up.

Refrain:

***Repeat refrain choreography**

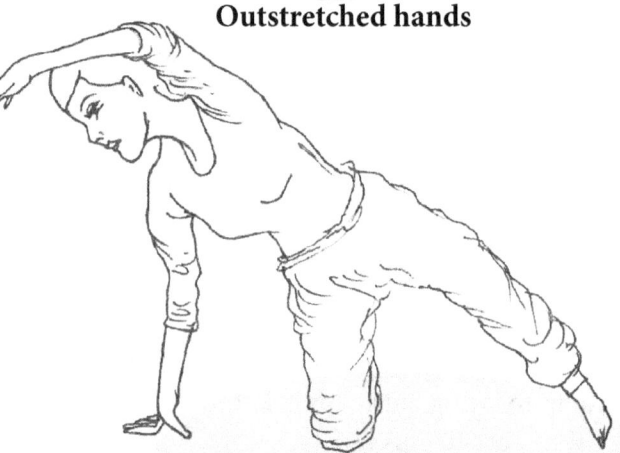

**Figure 15
Extend arm overhead
towards the center**

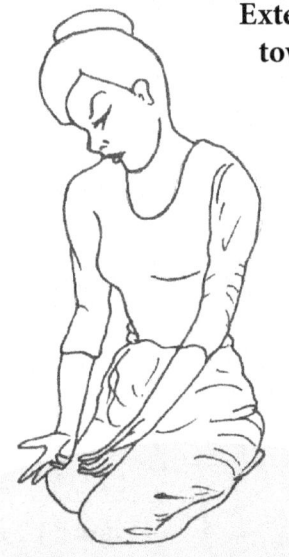

**Figure 16
Hands in lap**

OH, FREEDOM

Verse 1:

Oh freedom! Oh freedom! Oh freedom over me, when I am free.

Refrain:

    And befo' I'd be a slave
    I'll be buried in my grave
    An go home to my Lord and be free.

Verse 2:

No mo' moanin over me.

Refrain:

Verse 3:

There'll be singin' over me.

Refrain:

Verse 4:

There'll be prayin' over me.

Refrain:

Recommendations:
Up to 12 dancers, moderately slow tempo. Mood is full of yearning, and hopeful spirit.

Verse 1:

Oh, Freedom! Oh, Freedom! Oh, Freedom over me

Starting on right foot, dancers stride in a large clockwise circle, torso and left arm twisted right, left arm swinging back and down. **(fig. 1)**

**Figure 1
Long stride**

Refrain:

Choreography repeats throughout

An' befo' I'd be a slave

Dancers continue long strides, but contract torsos, hang heads and clasp hands behind their backs. **(fig. 2)**

**Figure 2
Slumping stride**

**Figure 3
Step forward on right foot**

I'll be buried in my grave.

Dancers swing hands up, then step forward on the right foot and lower the head and torso until both hands touch floor and left leg is lifted, pointing towards the ceiling. **(fig. 3)**

An' go home to my lord …

Bring feet together, bend the knees and roll up torso until straight, then reach head and arms high—torso pushing forward slightly. **(fig. 4)**

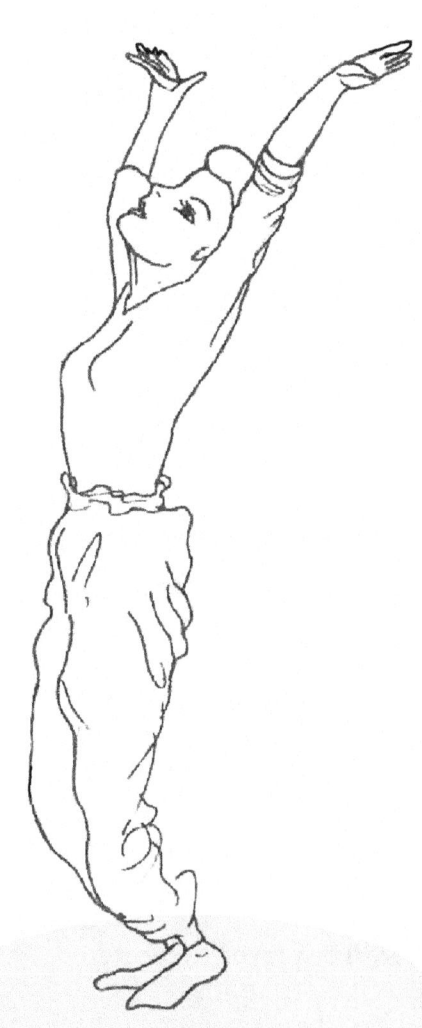

**Figure 4
Reaching up**

... and be free

Drop arms and with loose quick steps, walk in a clockwise circle, swinging opposite arms from the leading leg. (**fig. 5**)

Verse 2:

No mo' moanin', no mo' moanin', no mo' moanin over me
With trembling hands, cover face, then lower them while rounding torso until head hangs over slightly bent knees. (**figs. 6, 7**)

Refrain:

Repeat refrain choreography

Figure 5
Arms swing in opposition to legs

Figure 6
Trembling hands

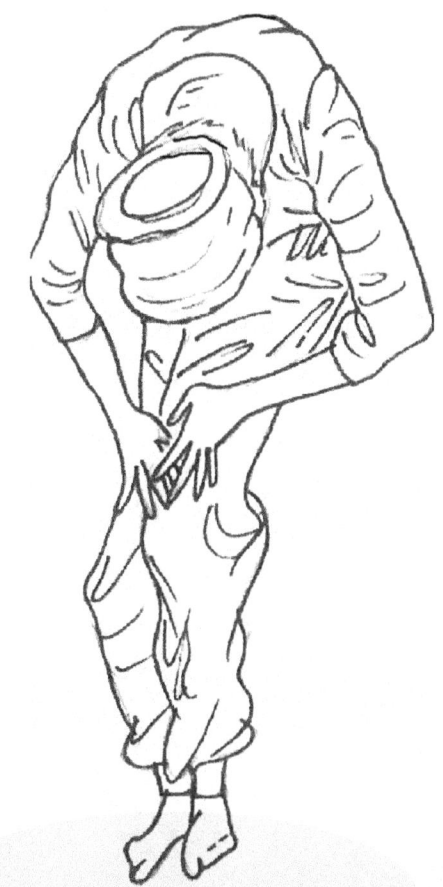

Figure 7
Rounded torso

Figure 8
Calling movement

Figure 9
Extend arms fully

Figure 5
Arms swing in opposition to legs

There'll be singin', there'll be singin', there'll be singin' over me.

Alternating between right and left, dancers take small side leaps, cupping hands to mouth and slowly extending them out. (figs. 8, 9) On the last "singin,'" turn in a circle to the right, swinging arms in opposition to their feet (right foot forward, left arm forward). **(fig. 5)**

Refrain:
Repeat refrain choreography

Verse 4:
There'll be prayin'…. There'll be prayin'… There'll be prayin' all over me.

Dancers turn a half circle to the right so their back faces the congregation. Clap in front of the chest and lift clasped hands overhead in a praying position. **(fig. 10)** Repeat, turning to face the congregation. The third time, circle arms backwards, clasp hands in prayer position, fingers touching chest, head leaning back, right leg extending into a backwards lunge.

Refrain:
Repeat refrain choreography

**Figure 10
Prayer position**

❋ HE'S GOT THE WHOLE WORLD IN HIS HANDS ❋

Feel the rhythm, He's got everybody; little bitty baby, you me, sun, moon, the whole world in his hands. Rejoice!

HE'S GOT THE WHOLE WORLD IN HIS HANDS

Verse 1:

He's got the whole world in His hands
He's got the whole world in His hands
He's got the big round world in His hands
He's got the whole world in His hands

Verse 2:

He's got the little bitty baby in His hands (3x)
He's got the whole world in His hands

Verse 3:

He's got you and me, sister, in His hands (3x)
He's got the whole world in His hands

Verse 4:

He's got you and me, brother, in His hands (3x)
He's got the whole world in His hands

Recommendations:
Up to 12 dancers. Tempo is upbeat and soulful. Props: Large beach ball

Starting position:
One dancer, holding a beachball over head, runs down the aisle to the chancel, then turns to face congregation. She leaps right, lands in a forward lunge with left foot extended behind, then lowers the ball to her waist. The dancer then rises with feet together and swings the ball first overhead, then to the left, before exiting to the right with quick. low running steps. The other dancers enter from and face congregation.

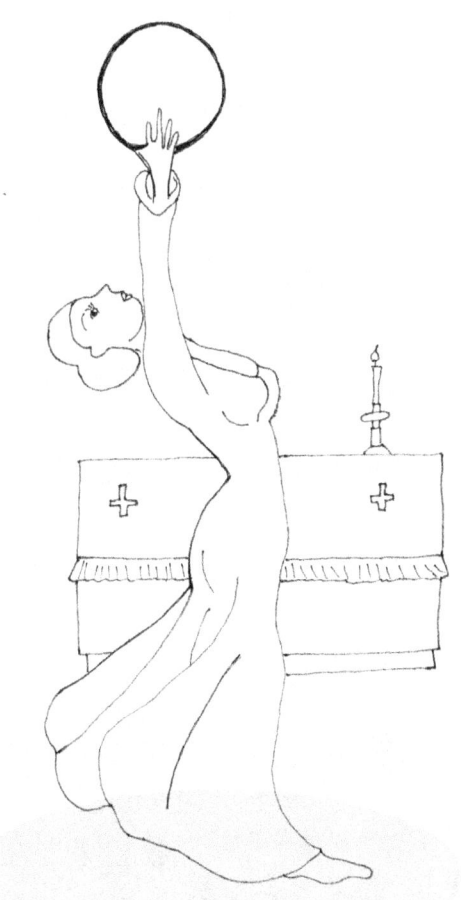

Figure 1
Starting Position

Verse 1:
He's got the whole world in His hands
Arms interlocked with a partner, dancers walk clockwise in relevé (on toes), facing the direction they are walking. **(fig. 2)**

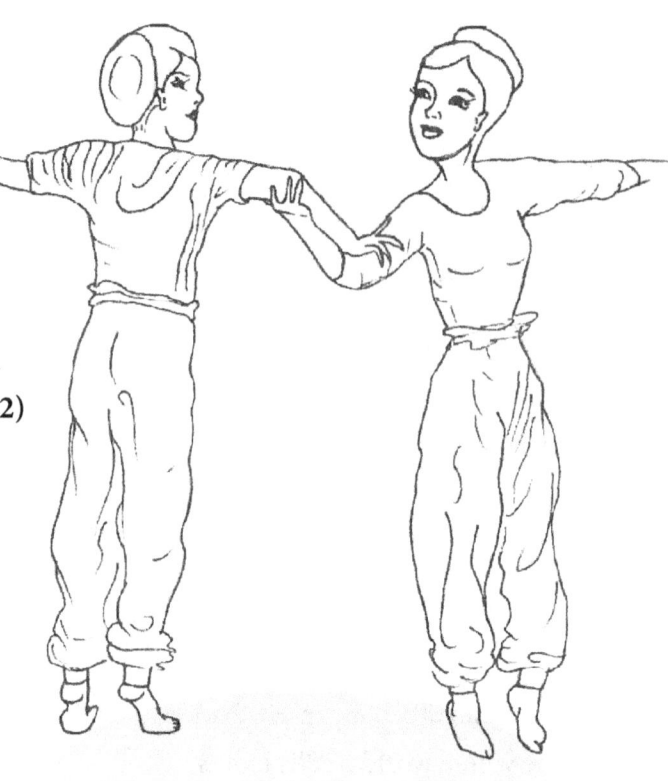

**Figure 2
Walking on Toes**

**Figure 3
Holding the world**

He's got the big round world
Still facing a partner, dancers lunge forward with right foot, then round arms, pull back torso and extend hands as if encircling a large globe. **(fig.3)**

in His hands
Still holding the world with outstretched hands and fingers, dancers circle entire torso to the right.

Figure 4
On toes, reaching up

He's got the whole world in His hands
*Choreography repeats for each verse
Bring feet together, sweep torso and arms in a large circle to the right, then bend torso and arms forward until fingers almost touch the ground. Roll up through the torso until standing on toes, reaching up. **(fig. 4)**

Verse 2:
He's got the little bitty baby in His hands (3x)
Dancers turn to face the congregation, arms in cradle position, rocking from side to side, faces focused on their arms. **(fig. 5)**

He's got the whole world in His hands
Repeat refrain choreography (fig. 4)

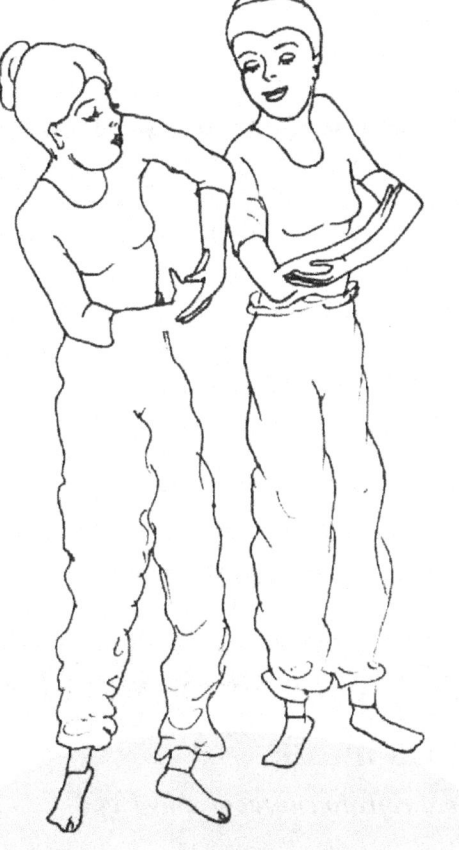

Figure 5
Cradling arms

Figure 6
Palms forward

Verse 3:

He's got you and me, sister, in His hands (3x)

Dancers walk a few steps forward, pointing to the congregation on "you", placing hands on their own chest on "me," and pushing flexed hands forward on "hands." **(fig. 6)**

He's got the whole world in His hands

Repeat refrain choreography (fig. 4)

Verse 4:

He's got you and me, brother

Dancers move in a low contracted turn to the left until they face a partner and grasp right arms above the elbow. **(fig. 7)**

in His hands. (3x)

Still partnered, dancers stand in relevé (on toes), round shoulders forward and focus on floor. On "hands," they focus on one another, lean and step back with outer leg, lift hands and raise their outside arms.

He's got the whole world in His hands

Repeat refrain choreography (fig.4)

Figure 7
Grasping arms above elbows

GO DOWN MOSES

Israel is the slave, Pharaoh the slave master, Moses from the mountain goes down the Mississippi with the slaves; let my people go.

GO DOWN MOSES

Verse 1:

When Israel was in Egypt's land, Let my people go.

Oppressed so hard they could not stand, Let my people go.

Refrain:

    Go down, Moses, Way down in Egypt land.

    Tell ole Pharaoh, Let my people go.

Verse 2:

Thus saith the Lord, "bold Moses said, Let my people go.

If not, I'll smite your first-born dead. Let my people go."

Refrain:

    Go down, Moses. Way down in Egypt land.

    Tell ole Pharaoh, Let my people go.

Recommendations:
One to twelve dancers, slow to moderate tempo, accompanied by a soloist, choir, ensemble or snare drums.

Starting Position:
Dancers stand with backs to one another, facing outward in a large circle. If there is only one dancer, their back is to the congregation. Feet are parallel, slightly apart, arms at sides, not touching the body, palms facing out. **(fig. 1)**

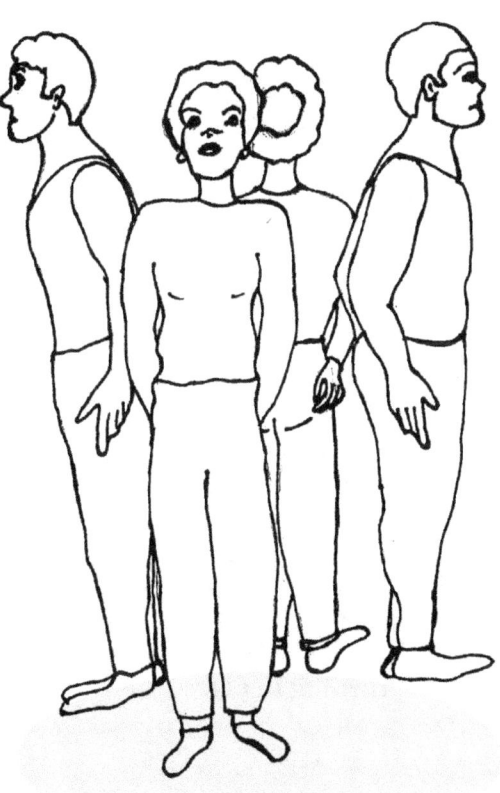

Figure 1
Backs to one another

When Israel was in Egypt's land

Leading with the right foot, every other dancer takes two small steps back and to the side to make pairs of dancers; one in front of the other. The front dancer lunges and swings arms in a right half circle around the dancer behind him/her. The rear dancer twists and swings his/her arms to the left, over the shoulders of the front dancer. (**fig.2**)

Let my people go

Crossing left foot over right, turn 180 degrees to the right, swinging arms and head up. On "people," contract forward while turning to complete circle, knees bent, arms and head down. (**fig. 3**) On "go," leap left, swinging arms left with hands outstretched above shoulders, landing with knees slightly bent in a centered wide stance, head and eyes down. (**fig. 4**)

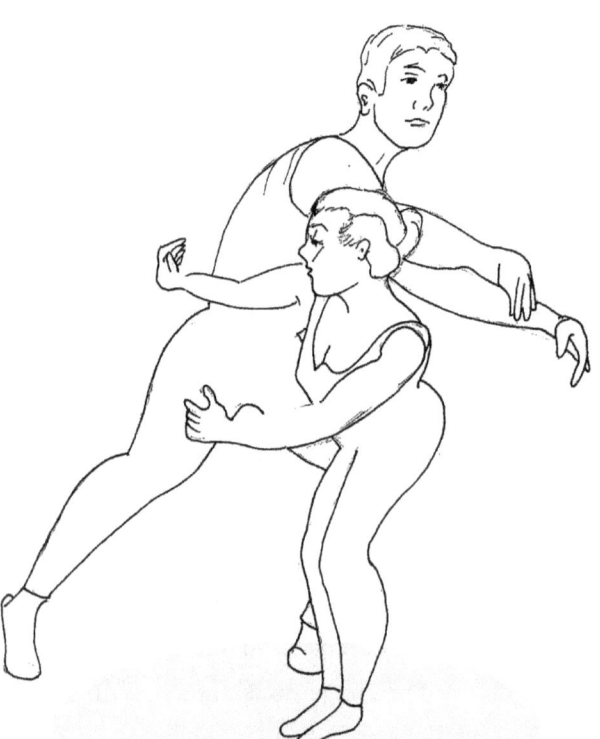

Figure 2
Dancers encircle one another

Figure 3
Turning in place

Figure 4
Leap with outstretched hands

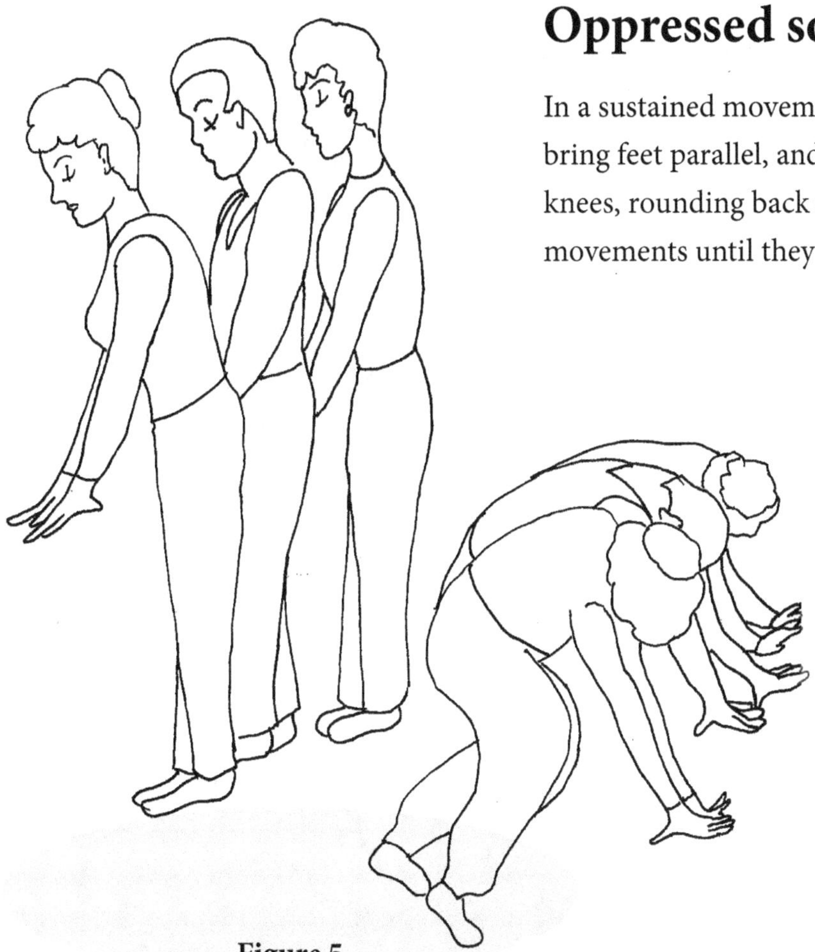

Oppressed so hard

In a sustained movement gazing down, turn slightly to the right, bring feet parallel, and continue to twist torso while bending knees, rounding back and pushing hands down in short repetitive movements until they are on the floor. (**fig. 5**)

Figure 5
Twist, bend, and lower

they could not stand

Dancers lean forward and rise to stand with feet together, pushing flexed hands out from chest, extending arms forward. (**Fig. 6**)

Let my people go
Repeat choreography (figs. 3, 4).

Figure 6
Rise to stand, pushing forward.

Figure 7
Dancers cluster, minus one

Refrain:

Go Down, Moses

Dancers move towards congregation, linking arms in a cluster. One dancer stands outside, facing group with arms extended, hands crossed. (**fig. 7**)

Figure 8
Pulling the dancer down

Way down in Egypt land

Dancers slowly pull the lone dancer by the arms and lower to their left knees. The standing dancer leans forward on right foot, lowering his/her torso, left leg extending back. (**fig. 8**)

Tell ole Pharaoh

All dancers (still in a circle) rise onto toes and bring hands to calling position, then extend hands out to the right, vibrating them at the end of the arms' full extension (**fig. 9**).

Figure 9
Calling position

"Let my people go!"

The group falls into a slight lunge, gazing down. Half the dancers' arms are crossed behind their heads, lunging to the left. The other half lunge forward with arms crossed over their chests. On "go," dancers swing arms and entire body upward, facing back into the circle. (**fig. 10**)

Figure 10
Dancers release upward

"Thus saith the Lord,"

Dancers turn to the right and drop to knees, placing hands on floor to the right of knees, facing down. (**fig. 11**)

Figure 11
Facing down

Bold Moses said

With right knee and hand still on floor and focusing gaze down, dancers extend left leg out to the side and place left hand over mouth. (**fig. 12**)

Figure 12
Extend left leg

Let my people go

Dancers sit back on heels and swing arms up on "go." **(fig. 13)**

If not, I'll smite

Dancers rise and step into a right forward lunge — leaning back, facing up— right arm swings up, left arm out. **(fig. 14a)**

your first-born dead

Dancers fall into a deep contraction, shoulders rounded, head and knees bent, feet parallel, fingers touching the floor. **(fig. 14b)**

Let my people go

Still bent, dancers bring hands to body's center, slowing turn towards the left and step forward on the right foot, so right knee is bent and left leg extends back, heel slightly off the floor. On "go", forcefully swing arms to sides at shoulder height, **(fig. 14c, 14d)**

Figure 13
Swing up arms

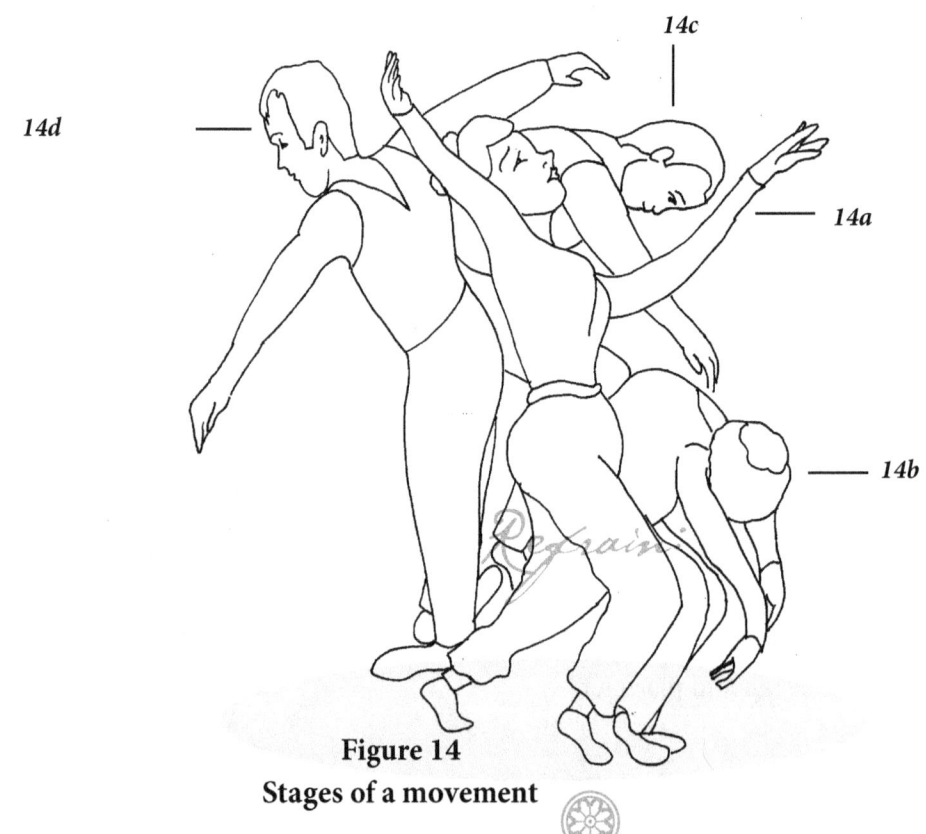

Figure 14
Stages of a movement

Refrain:
Repeat refrain choreography

Let my people go

Dancers do a deep left lunge, heel off the floor, right leg extended with toes pointed, leaning back. Right arm extends back, interlocking with arm of dancer behind. **(fig. 15)** On "go," left arm extends up, interlocking with wrist of dancer behind, head follows all movements to end focusing up. **(fig. 16)**

Figure 15
Lunge with interlocking arms

Figure 16
Final left lunge with interlocking arms

ACKNOWLEDGEMENTS

MY MOTHER, LAURA BUCK MCCRAY, WHO LAID THE FOUNDATION FOR MY LOVE OF DANCE, AND INTRODUCED ME TO THE POSSIBILITES OF LITURGICAL DANCE.

My late husband, Rev. Fletcher Juan Bryant, who encouraged and nurtured this project from its infancy.

My three children, who never tired in their support on this journey: Anthony gave me a spiritual push whenever I needed it; Shanta Bryant Gyan was sometimes my editor, sometimes my publicist, and in the home stretch, she compiled the stellar editorial and design team that brought the book to completion; Laura Bryant Njanga's goal-setting and encouragement kept me on track when I faltered.

My sons-in-law, Joel Eddy Njanga, who nourished and sustained our family through his care and love for the project; and Albert Gyan, who encouraged me to keep my focus throughout the journey.

My editor, Gillian Aldrich, for her excellent editorial insight, and for tapping her inner dancer to translate my compositions to the page. Gillian is also an award winning video and radio producer.

Heather Kern, for my book's stunningly cohesive design. Her company, Pop Shop Studios, has completed award-winning designs for clients in print, online, interactive multimedia, photography, illustration and environmental design.

Mary Jane Airel, whose elegant line illustrations infused my choreography with lyrical clarity. She even put down her pen to dance alongside me in order to better understand the movements.

Photographers Susie Adamson and Julian Espinal. In different ways, their stunning photographs manage to capture the movement and spirit of my compositions. Maria de L. Rivera, for her insightful photo editing, and Diana Sherblom, for the wonderful family portrait.

Reverend Gene Hamilton, United Methodist Elder, evangelist and artist; for the creative expressions that proceed each composition.

Bernadette Abeywickrama, for editorial assistance.

Finally, I am thankful that God has given me the gift to glorify and praise Him through dance, and to share that gift with others. What an amazing grace!

ABOUT THE AUTHOR

Sylvia Buck Bryant is an accomplished dancer, teacher and choreographer in sacred and contemporary dance. In addition to holding a Bachelors from Tuskegee University and Masters of Science from George Peabody College of Vanderbilt University, Bryant attended the American Dance Festival at Connecticut College of Dance in New London, Conn where she was introduced to, and studied with Martha Graham, Rod Rodgers, José Limón and Charles Weidman— all pioneers of contemporary dance. Bryant also studied with the Alvin Ailey American Theater, George Faison, and Margaret Fisk Taylor-Doane, who put sacred dance on the map. In addition to choreographing, teaching and performing liturgical dance in churches ministered by her husband, the late Reverend Fletcher Juan Bryant, for over 30 years, Mrs. Bryant directed the dance programs at Fisk University in Nashville, Tennessee, and Philander Smith College in Little Rock, Arkansas. She has performed in numerous professional venues in New York, Baltimore, and London. One of the highlights of her dance career was being invited to dance at Wesley Chapel in London, England. Her first published book of sacred dance, *Dancing Through The Christian Calendar* (Cokesbury, 1996) established her position as a pre-eminent liturgical choreographer. In 2013 she was invited to participate in a community piece choreographed by Ronald K. Brown, of Evidence, A Dance Company, at BRIC House in Brooklyn. That same year, she traveled to Nairobi, Kenya where she was a guest artist in a tribute performance for Dr. Maya Angelou at the Paa Ya Paa Arts Center, founded by Phillda and Elimo Njau.

In addition to working as the Montclair School District's Parent Liaison Coordinator in New Jersey, Bryant continues to choreograph, teach, and perform, as the founder and director of the Call to Worship Liturgical Dance Ensemble, which travels and performs throughout the U.S.

ABOUT THE ILLUSTRATOR

Mary Jane Airel is a wildlife muralist, painter, and illustrator. Her murals are on permanent display in corporate headquarters in the New York metropolitan area, and her portraits can be found in collections throughout the United States and Europe. Ms. Ariel has also penned and illustrated three children's books and is sought after for her pet portraits. Her painting, "In Remembrance," a tribute to the families of those who perished on September 11, 2001, was distributed nationwide. She resides with her husband, son, and Yorkshire terrier in Tom's River, New Jersey.